INSIDE THE INDUSTRY
ENGINEERING

BY SUSAN E. HAMEN

Content Consultant
Cynthia L. Favre
Director of Career Management
Gustavus Adolphus College

ABDO
Publishing Company

CREDITS

Published by ABDO Publishing Company, 8000 West 78th Street, Edina, Minnesota 55439. Copyright © 2011 by Abdo Consulting Group, Inc. International copyrights reserved in all countries. No part of this book may be reproduced in any form without written permission from the publisher. The Essential Library™ is a trademark and logo of ABDO Publishing Company.

Printed in the United States of America,
North Mankato, Minnesota
112010
012011

♲ THIS BOOK CONTAINS AT LEAST 10% RECYCLED MATERIALS.

Editor: Holly Saari
Copy Editor: Susan Freese
Interior Design and Production: Christa Schneider
Cover Design: Christa Schneider

Library of Congress Cataloging-in-Publication Data
Hamen, Susan E.
  Engineering / by Susan E. Hamen.
     p. cm. -- (Inside the industry)
  Includes bibliographical references and index.
  ISBN 978-1-61714-798-2
  1. Engineering--Vocational guidance--Juvenile literature. I. Title.
  TA157.H27 2011
  620.0023--dc22
                                    2010044460

TABLE OF CONTENTS

Chapter 1	Is an Engineering Job for You?	6
Chapter 2	What Is a Chemical Engineer?	14
Chapter 3	Would You Make a Good Chemical Engineer?	26
Chapter 4	What Is an Environmental Engineer?	34
Chapter 5	Would You Make a Good Environmental Engineer?	44
Chapter 6	What Is a Computer Engineer?	54
Chapter 7	Would You Make a Good Computer Engineer?	66
Chapter 8	What Is a Video Game Developer?	76
Chapter 9	Would You Make a Good Video Game Developer?	88

Get Your Foot in the Door 96

Professional Organizations 98

Market Facts 100

Glossary 102

Additional Resources 104

Source Notes 106

Index 110

About the Author 112

Engineers design plans for windmills and other structures that impact our daily lives.

IS AN ENGINEERING JOB FOR YOU?

"Scientists investigate that which already is; engineers create that which has never been."[1]
—*Albert Einstein (1879–1955), physicist*

You really love science and math. Physics and chemistry may be your best subjects. You have thought about how humans impact the earth and understand the need for clean air and water. Perhaps you love computers and spend most of your free time on your laptop. You like to take things apart and rebuild them simply to figure out how they work. Maybe your favorite activity is playing video games, and you are fascinated by the detail of the games and their characters.

As you look to the future, you wonder how you can turn your love of these things into a career. Perhaps you have considered the field of engineering. You have heard of electrical, civil, computer, and chemical engineers, but what exactly do they do? What skill set do you need for each? And how do you become an engineer?

DEFINITION OF ENGINEERING

Engineering is "the application of science and mathematics by which the properties of matter and the sources of energy in nature are made useful to people."[2] The word *engineer* comes from the Latin word *ingeniator*, which means "the ingenious one."

A WORLD OF POSSIBILITIES

Engineering is an old and diverse field. The early Romans used environmental and civil engineering to create aqueducts that provided clean water to the city. The Egyptian pyramids, the Greek Parthenon, and the Great Wall of China are all historic examples of extraordinary works of engineering. Even catapults and crossbows were the handiwork of engineers using principles that would later translate into military engineering.

ENGINEERING AND LEONARDO DA VINCI

Early engineers did not have a degree or a formal education. Rather, they invented devices or tools through tinkering, imagination, and trial and error. Leonardo da Vinci was an engineer in Italy in the fifteenth and sixteenth centuries. His note-books show drawings of machines and instruments, including some intended for use in war and human flight.

Look around you. Engineers help to create the things you use every single day, including roads, buildings, alarm clocks, MP3 players, laptops, and cars. Laundry detergent, soap, shampoo, and plastic are also products created by engineers. Even water is processed and cleaned with equipment and chemicals designed by engineers.

The environments that engineers work in are as diverse as the things they create. Engineers can work for different types and sizes of employers, independently as consultants, and at universities and research facilities.

Today, engineering is a particularly good field for women. Because men have traditionally dominated the industry, many scholarships and other opportunities are now offered to women in the hope of drawing them to the field.

CHOOSING YOUR PATH

To decide if engineering is the career path for you, you should consider several questions about this kind of work. For

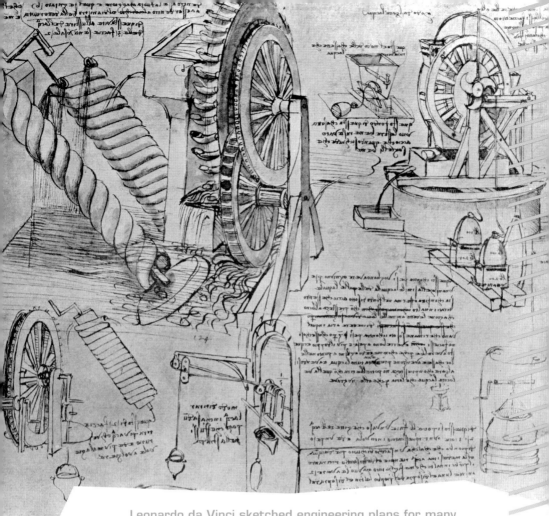

Leonardo da Vinci sketched engineering plans for many inventions, including water-raising devices.

example, are you comfortable working with others, or would you rather work alone? Engineers often work on projects as a team. Do you like using science and math to problem solve and to come up with new ideas and answers? Is accuracy important to you? Engineers like science and are often very detail oriented.

What type of engineering is most appealing to you? Automotive engineers design and build cars. Computer

"[Engineering] is a great profession. There is the satisfaction of watching a figment of the imagination emerge through the aid of science to a plan on paper. Then it moves to realization in stone or metal or energy. . . . It elevates the standards of living and adds to the comforts of life. This is the engineer's high privilege. . . . To the engineer falls the job of clothing the bare bones of science with life, comfort and hope."[3]

—*Herbert Hoover, thirty-first president of the United States and professional mining engineer*

engineers develop software and build computers. Chemical engineers create and improve products that range from paint to explosives. But this is only a sampling of the many areas of engineering. Whenever science and mathematics are used to design, build, or create, some type of engineering is involved.

TEN POPULAR ENGINEERING JOBS

This book will introduce you to four engineering professions: chemical, environmental, and computer engineering and video game developing. Here are ten other popular professions in the engineering industry:

1. Aerospace engineer: Aerospace engineers specialize in developing new technologies for use in aviation, defense systems, and space exploration. They often work in areas such as structural design, guidance, navigation and control, and instrumentation and communication.

2. Civil engineer: Civil engineers design and supervise the construction of roads, buildings, airports, tunnels, dams, bridges, and water supply and sewage systems.

3. Electrical engineer: Electrical engineers design, develop, test, and supervise the manufacture of electrical equipment, including machinery controls, radar systems, automobile and aircraft electrical designs, and communications systems.

4. Electronics engineer: Electronics engineers work with a wide range of technologies, from portable music players to global positioning systems. They are responsible for the design, development, and testing of electronic equipment, and they oversee the manufacturing process.

5. Health and safety engineer: Health and safety engineers identify potential safety hazards in buildings and other structures by using knowledge of mechanical, chemical, or structural engineering. They try to reduce the risk of fires, toxin exposures, accidents, and other hazards.

6. Industrial engineer: Industrial engineers decide the most effective ways to use people, machines, materials, information, and energy to produce a product or provide a service.

7. Materials engineer: Materials engineers develop, process, and test materials for a wide variety

of products. The metals, ceramics, plastics, semiconductors, and other materials they help create are used for such items as computer chips, golf clubs, television screens, and skis.

8. Mechanical engineer: Mechanical engineers work on researching, designing, developing, manufacturing, and testing tools, engines, and many other mechanical devices.

9. Nuclear engineer: Nuclear engineers research and develop ways to harness nuclear energy and radiation as power sources. Some might design, develop, and help run nuclear power plants.

10. Petroleum engineer: Petroleum engineers develop the methods used for extracting oil and natural gas. With geologists, they determine the properties of the rock and soil from which the petroleum will be extracted. They decide on a proper drilling method, and they design drilling processes and equipment.

NUMBER OF ENGINEERS

In 2008, engineers held approximately 1.6 million jobs in the United States. Civil engineers made up the largest group, with 278,400 employed. The next-largest group was mechanical engineers, with 238,700 employed, followed by industrial engineers, with 214,800 employed. Approximately 12 percent of all engineers are employed by federal, state, or local governments.[4]

Some computer engineers design and build computers.

Some chemical engineers spend time working in laboratories.

WHAT IS A CHEMICAL ENGINEER?

You need only look around your house to see the work of chemical engineers. Do you have toothpaste, shampoo, shaving cream, cosmetics, or lotion in the bathroom? Do you have cleaning products, such as detergents and disinfectants, in the kitchen or the laundry room? Do the shelves in the garage contain motor oil, antifreeze, or windshield washer fluid? Does anyone in your family garden and use fertilizers, pest control, or plant food? How many of the things you own are made of plastic? All of these things—and many more everyday items—are designed by chemical engineers.

Massachusetts Institute of Technology (MIT), a university located in Cambridge, Massachusetts, is a world leader in scientific and technological research. MIT's Department of Chemical Engineering states, "Chemical engineering is about transformation. It's about gaining fundamental knowledge about a substance, then using that knowledge to synthesize a solution to an important medical, mechanical, or societal need."[1]

Chemical engineers work in many areas, which means students have many choices of career paths. Because of this, chemical engineering is sometimes called the "liberal arts of engineering."[2] Some chemical engineers choose to specialize in a certain area, such as food engineering, biochemical engineering, petrochemical engineering, pharmaceuticals, or paper and textile production. Some chemical engineers help develop food additives and preservatives that lengthen the life and quality of food. Others help develop pesticides and fertilizers that keep food crops disease free and pest resistant.

In sum, chemical engineers help produce products that fill a need or answer an everyday problem. Typically, chemists working in laboratories invent or improve a certain product—

for example, a new type of whitening toothpaste. A chemical engineer then builds on the chemist's findings to design an industrial process to produce the toothpaste on a large scale in a safe, efficient, and cost-effective manner.

Chemical engineers often work in plants that produce everything from paint, dye, and plastics to fertilizers, glue, and perfume. Engineers are also responsible for developing the design of the plant, customizing the software used in the design, and planning the equipment within the plant. Some engineers find ways to improve plant operations.

For any production plant to be successful, it must be efficient and economical yet also follow strict safety procedures. It's often the job of chemical

"Chemical engineering has been around for over 100 years . . . and has made numerous contributions to the fabric of our industrial society. Chemical engineers produce fertilizers that have been responsible for eradicating hunger in the world; they produce fuels like gasoline that power the engine of our society; they produce the plastics and metals that are in most things we use; they produce cement that has made possible the cities we live in; they produce fibers that clothe us; they produce the chips that power our computers; they produce the processed food that stocks the shelves of our grocery stores; and they produce the pharmaceuticals that keep us healthy. Chemical engineers are involved in every process involving chemistry in the commercial sector. The modern life would not be possible without the contributions of chemical engineers."[3]

—Worcester Polytechnic Institute Department of Chemical Engineering engineers to ensure the plant operates effectively and safely. Chemical engineers often write safety procedures and protocols to ensure plant employees work in the safest possible environment.

Chemical engineers also have the added challenge of devising safe ways to handle the dangerous by-products of chemical manufacturing. After you repaint your bedroom or change the oil in your car, what do you do with the mostly empty paint cans or used oil? It is unsafe to dump these things down the drain or throw them away. Harmful chemicals must be disposed of properly, in a way that won't harm humans or the environment. Chemical engineers face similar problems on a daily basis. They must make sure that manufacturing processes and products are safe for production workers and product users and that production has no ill effects on the environment.

WHAT IS A CHEMICAL ENGINEER'S WORK ENVIRONMENT?

Many chemical engineers work in a chemical-processing plant. In a plant, machines can be very loud, so wearing hearing protection is necessary. Safety shoes and gloves are worn as well. In areas that contain dangerous fumes, engineers and other employees wear protective bodysuits, with breathing devices designed to filter out harmful fumes. Other chemical engineers work in a laboratory, where they collaborate with chemists on research and development. Some engineers advance to management positions and work in office settings.

Petrochemical engineers find better ways to refine oil and natural gas.

Chemical engineers at plants typically work in teams with other engineers. In most cases, they work a standard 40-hour workweek. However, because plants usually run 24 hours a day, chemical engineers might receive a phone call at night or over the weekend if something unexpected happens at the plant.

Some chemical engineers, especially those who work in the oil refinery business, travel extensively. They visit different work sites, both within the country and abroad, to oversee operations and to troubleshoot problems.

HOW IS THE JOB MARKET FOR CHEMICAL ENGINEERS?

In 2008, approximately 31,700 chemical engineers worked in the United States.[4] Their average starting salary was $63,616.[5] The median salary was $84,680 a year.[6]

A decline of about 2 percent is predicted in the number of chemical engineering jobs between 2008 and 2018.[7] Economic factors will likely contribute to a decline in the manufacture and sale of chemicals, which will mean fewer chemical plants operating and fewer engineers working. However, forecasters predict more opportunities for chemical engineering positions that focus on energy research, biotechnology, and environmental issues.

A PROFILE OF A CHEMICAL ENGINEER

As a former project engineer, Jason Trask helped plan and manage the installation of large-scale equipment and structures in his plant. These included conveyor systems, product storage tanks, and pipe systems. In his new position, he is an environmental, health, and safety manager for CHS Oilseed Processing and Refining, a soybean-processing plant located in Mankato, Minnesota, a city with approximately 30,000 people. Trask is responsible for developing and managing programs that ensure safe work sites and prevent harmful effects to the environment and the community.

In a typical day, Trask spends a lot of time in his office, working on a computer. He also meets with colleagues and employees in the plant. Together, they ensure tasks are prioritized and executed so that production deadlines are met. Juggling many tasks and dealing with unexpected issues are both part of Trask's daily routine. "The work is very diverse and ever changing," he explained. "Being self-motivated and directed, as well as detail oriented, is essential for success in this position."[8]

"Unlike most fields, the job options are immense and there are way too many to list here. A chemical engineering degree is highly regarded in most industries and is seen as an excellent educational background as well as a positive indicator for strong future performance. A chemical engineering degree, along with a good work history, can create high-level job opportunities even outside the engineering field. For example, my supervisor has a chemical engineering degree, and he is in the job position of vice president of operations."[9]

—Jason Trask, chemical engineer, CHS Oilseed Processing and Refining

Looking back to college, Trask recalls that one of his most memorable classes was about plant design. He and his fellow students were required to complete a preliminary design of a manufacturing plant. Trask explained, "The work was similar to what an engineer could be expected to do on the job. The class required us to combine and utilize much of what we learned in all of our other engineering classes."[10] By taking this class, Trask discovered his passion and turned it into his career.

FACT OR FICTION?

One popular story from the history of chemical engineering is about Ivory soap, a soap that floats. Legend has it that in the late nineteenth century, an employee at Proctor & Gamble forgot to shut off his soap-making machine when he went on his lunch break. When he returned, the soap mixture was frothy and puffy, but he finished the soap as usual. It was later shipped out. Soon, customers contacted Proctor & Gamble saying they wanted more "floating soap." According to Proctor & Gamble, "Whether by chance or intentional discovery, . . . floating soap has set Ivory's purity apart for more than a century."[11]

A DAY IN THE LIFE OF A CHEMICAL ENGINEER

Since chemical engineers work with such a broad range of products and processes, their daily responsibilities can vary greatly. However, a typical chemical engineer who works in a plant spends part of the day observing operations and assessing whether improvements can be made in the

BECOME A GREEN ENGINEER

The US Environmental Protection Agency (EPA) is an agency of the federal government that enforces regulations and laws passed by Congress to protect human and environmental health. The EPA employs chemical engineers for its Green Engineering Team. The team's goal is to "institutionalize green thinking in the design and commercialization of products and processes."[12] Green thinking is an approach to conserving natural resources and improving the state of the environment.

production process. The engineer takes precise measurements and analyzes them to correctly predict the outcome of production projects. He or she is responsible for preparing multiple reports that detail the findings of tests and evaluations.

Engineers also monitor any irregularities in test results; a simple change in temperature or pressure can affect production and end up costing the plant thousands of dollars. Engineers must also investigate why the irregularities occurred. Chemical engineers spend time answering the question how?

Chemical engineers also spend a lot of time every day at a computer. They input data and analyze information, manage safety issues, and track compliance with applicable laws and safety regulations.

A chemical engineer often wears protective gear, such as a hard hat and safety goggles.

THE TOP FIVE QUESTIONS ABOUT BECOMING A CHEMICAL ENGINEER

1. *How many years of college education will I need?*
   The profession almost always requires a chemical engineering degree. Earning a bachelor's of science degree in chemical engineering will take four or five years, depending on what university you attend. Earning a master's degree will take another two or three years.

2. *I love chemistry, but I struggle with math. Is it possible to get a chemical engineering degree without taking math classes?*
   All chemical engineering degrees require extensive math courses. Making calculations and taking measurements are crucial parts of an engineer's daily routine. Look into getting a tutor to assist you with your math homework. Consider taking basic math classes to build a strong foundation of math concepts, which will prepare you for more challenging math classes.

3. *What can I do in high school to get a jump start on a degree in chemical engineering?*

    Take all the math and science courses you can. The more you learn about science and math in high school, the better you will do in college-level courses. If your school has a chemistry or science club, join it.

4. *After I earn my college degree, will I be done with my education?*

    After completing a college education, most engineers take tests and become licensed. They also continue their education through conferences, seminars, and classes to stay current on information related to their areas of specialty.

5. *How safe is a job as a chemical engineer?*

    Chemical engineers work with chemicals that may be hazardous. Some engineers work in plants that produce explosives or toxic chemicals. However, safety precautions are taken. Chemical engineering is not considered a hazardous job.

If you love chemistry, chemical engineering may be a good career path for you.

WOULD YOU MAKE A GOOD CHEMICAL ENGINEER?

D o you think chemical engineering might be for you? Are you wondering if you would be successful in this field? Most chemical engineers share some key interests and skills that lead to success in their jobs.

LOVE OF MATH AND SCIENCE

Chemical engineers spend most of their day deep in scientific and mathematical thought. Many recall enjoying a variety of math and science classes—especially chemistry—throughout high school and college. However, chemical engineering is about more than just enjoying academics. Chemical engineers *apply* their knowledge of chemistry, math, and other scientific principles to troubleshoot or improve on plant processes.

HAVING PROBLEM-SOLVING, ANALYSIS, AND RESEARCH SKILLS

Chemical engineers in many different job settings also rely heavily on superior problem-solving abilities. They must be able to use critical-thinking skills to come up with solutions and processes. Because engineers also analyze daily processes, diagrams, tables, and equations,

"The ability to create products from chemical reactions is something that I found amazing as a student in high school. Also, chemical engineering has such a wide variety of applications. I wanted to be in a major where I had a lot of options. I could be working for a pharmaceutical company, making silicon wafers for electronics, making gas out of oil, and even making cosmetics. There are so many different things you can do with a chemical engineering degree."[1]

—*Janice Mathew, chemical engineering student at MIT*

Chemical engineers need to work well with others.

they must have superb analytical skills to be successful. In many cases, chemical engineers have to perform research to gather the necessary information to improve processes. Doing so requires good research skills.

BEING DETAIL ORIENTED

Chemical engineers are good at noticing details. They must monitor the entire production process, and if one small piece isn't working correctly or at optimum efficiency, they must find it and correct it. Even the smallest flaw in calculations can change the outcome of production.

WORKING IN A TEAM

Chemical engineers rarely work alone. They work on teams with other engineers, supervisors from other areas of the plant, and production workers. Chemical engineers are in constant communication with these people to ensure processes are running smoothly and safely. While chemical engineers don't need to be outgoing or sociable, their work environment is definitely not private or quiet.

CHECKLIST

Are you a good candidate for a career in chemical engineering? Use this checklist to help you decide if you have the right skills and personal qualities:

- *Are you good at problem solving, and do you like puzzles?*

- *Do you have excellent chemistry and math skills?*

- *Do you like building things?*

- *Do you like coming up with better and more efficient ways of doing things?*

- *Do you like figuring out how small pieces come together to form one large working unit?*

- *Do you pay attention to small details?*

If you answered yes to the majority of these questions, then you might have the skills needed to become a chemical engineer. If you lack some of these skills, don't rule out chemical engineering as a profession. Hard work and determination can take you a long way toward achieving your dream career.

HOW TO GET THERE

IN HIGH SCHOOL

While you are in high school, consider getting a jump start on acquiring some of the skills needed in chemical engineering. Take challenging math and science classes, such as calculus and chemistry. If your high school offers Advanced Placement (AP) or honors courses in science or math, take them. Having knowledge of these subjects at an advanced level will only help you once you are in college. Remember, many chemical engineers have to create tables and spreadsheets of complex data, so taking extra computer classes will be beneficial, as well. In addition, chemical engineers often have to write reports, so take advantage of writing courses, too.

If your school has a science club, it's a good idea to join it. Participating in a program with like-minded people will give you a boost that will help you in your college courses. If your school doesn't offer such a club, consider starting one or joining an online club.

In addition, go to the library and check out books and magazines about chemistry and engineering. Read blogs and other Web sites devoted to engineering. It's never too early to start learning about your possible career path.

REQUIRED EDUCATION

Chemical engineers need to earn at least a bachelor's degree in chemical engineering. Some engineers—especially those who wish to work in research and development—continue on to earn a master's degree or a doctorate (PhD). A master's degree typically requires two years of coursework and writing a thesis or completing a special in-depth project. Another two to four years is needed to earn a PhD.

In addition to a degree, a chemical engineer who wants to provide services to the public must be licensed. Licensure requires earning a bachelor's degree from an accredited university, having relevant work experience, and passing a state examination.

COLLEGE COURSES

The coursework required to earn a chemical engineering degree can be tough. Typically, students must complete several advanced calculus and chemistry classes before beginning chemical engineering classes. Many students take advantage of tutoring and study groups offered by their college or university.

Required courses for the major can include biomolecular engineering, quantum mechanics, and chemical engineering process design. Students also take classes that address specific types of chemical engineering, such as food process engineering, genetics, tissue engineering, water and wastewater treatment, polymers, renewable energy, and chemistry of plant materials. Students must also take classes that require spending time in a laboratory.

JOIN A CLUB

Many colleges have engineering clubs or organizations students can join. They provide excellent opportunities to meet others and work on the skills needed by chemical engineers. Members get to participate in such benefits as attending conferences, where they can hear speakers from the industry share their experiences and knowledge. In addition, members may attend onsite plant visits, participate in presenting collaborative projects, and socialize with others who share the same passion for chemical engineering. The extra experience you gain from club and organization projects will look good to potential employers on your résumé. However, you will also need to be able to state clearly in an interview what you got out of the experience and how it relates to your career interest. Belonging to such groups is also a great way to develop your interpersonal and communication skills. Additionally, being active in extracurricular activities such as these helps you network with people who might be able to help you find a job following graduation.

AN EXAMPLE CLASS

Lynn Reuvers, a chemical engineer with nearly 30 years of experience, remembers her early, exciting days as a chemical engineer: "We were working with chemicals [polymers] that we hoped would result in a plastic that was temperature resistant and strong enough to make engine blocks out of. We were also improving 'Lexan,' the plastic used in banks and walkways to thwart bullets. I even shot bullets at a few blocks of Lexan during testing!"[2]

An internship can help you gain experience and begin networking.

INTERNSHIPS

After completing the coursework for a chemical engineering degree at a university, students often do an internship. An intern gains practical experience working under a chemical engineer in a work setting. Internships usually pay a low wage or no wage at all, but they can often lead to full-time employment.

Environmental engineers may work outside, in places such as solar power stations, or in laboratories.

WHAT IS AN ENVIRONMENTAL ENGINEER?

Environmental engineers apply the principles of chemistry and biology to prevent or to resolve problems with the quality of water, air, and land. These engineers also study the effects of humans on the planet:

How is the environment affected by logging and building? How do toxic fertilizers and pesticides harm groundwater? How are human population and the use of resources impacting ecosystems around the world? How does pollution affect animals? These are some questions environmental engineers try to answer.

Environmental engineers are a key part of managing pollution and the effects of building and developing in communities. Many environmental engineers help their clients find ways to deal with hazardous waste. This could include helping a contractor or manufacturing plant dispose of industrial wastewater, toxic chemicals, or other by-products. Environmental engineers also address the problems of acid rain, ozone depletion, and air pollution from automobile exhaust and industry. In addition, they work to develop laws and regulations for the disposal of hazardous waste. Unfortunately, environmental engineers sometimes have the hard task of helping to create solutions for environmental accidents, such as oil spills in the ocean. This can require helping to create completely new technologies.

Environmental engineers monitor the processes that clean and treat water for human consumption. They are responsible for designing sewer systems that carry waste material from homes and buildings to a collection site, where it's treated before being discharged into rivers, lakes, or oceans. These engineers also help design water distribution systems that deliver pressurized water to the taps in people's homes. They often work alongside civil engineers to plan and design these systems.

THE IMPORTANCE OF CLEAN WATER

It has been said that civil and environmental engineers have saved more lives than all of the doctors in the world combined because these engineers have provided people with safe drinking water and sanitation. However, many people around the world still don't have clean drinking water. According to the United Nations Environment Programme, "The sheer scale of dirty water means more people now die from contaminated and polluted water than from all forms of violence including wars."[1]

Environmental engineers help monitor groundwater quality in areas near landfills, and they work to prevent unnecessary erosion in landfill areas. They also help safely close landfills and assist with the design of new alternatives for waste disposal.

Environmental engineers often specialize in a certain field, such as water treatment, soil erosion, or global warming. Some are self-employed and work as consultants, while others work for environmental engineering firms or companies that hire engineers to oversee proper waste disposal. The government hires environmental engineers to help enforce laws and regulations.

WHAT IS AN ENVIRONMENTAL ENGINEER'S WORK ENVIRONMENT?

Environmental engineers work in laboratories, in the outdoors, or a combination of the two. Some engineers need access to a full chemical laboratory to run tests on samples to check for pollutants. The engineers who work outdoors collect samples and perform tests on water and soil. Some might investigate and monitor damage caused by off-road vehicles.

Environmental engineers' site visits aren't usually to beautiful, pristine settings. Typically, these visits are to unpleasant surroundings that may be contaminated with chemicals, pollution, and other products. Some environmental engineers who perform research travel to distant areas of the globe, such as Antarctica and the North Pole, to study the effects of pollution or ozone depletion on climate.

Some environmental engineers who travel outside the United States work in developing countries that have poor water treatment facilities. Environmental engineers may work with local governments and communities to remedy this problem. These engineers help design and construct sewage and irrigation systems and construct drinkable water sources and systems. Then they train people how to operate and manage the newly constructed facilities.

Often, environmental engineers work as members of a team of professionals that might include a civil engineer, a geologist, or a field technician. Even engineers who work primarily as consultants must be prepared to collaborate with others. In addition to working with others, environmental engineers often speak to clients, possibly giving presentations.

Collaborating with other engineers is an important part of being an environmental engineer.

HOW IS THE JOB MARKET FOR ENVIRONMENTAL ENGINEERS?

Approximately 54,300 environmental engineers were employed in the United States in 2008. On average, environmental engineers earned $74,020 a year.[2]

Although job opportunities in many career areas have dwindled due to the economic recession, the US Department of Labor predicts a 31 percent increase in the number of jobs for environmental engineers by the year 2018.[3] According to a 2005 report by *Fortune* magazine,

> *The greatest increase in demand [in the job market] by far will be for folks who know how to clean up . . . earth. . . . An increasingly health-conscious public is eager to find*

environmental engineers who can prevent problems rather than simply control those that already exist.[4]

PROFILE OF AN ENVIRONMENTAL ENGINEER

After ten years as an environmental consultant, George Beatty decided to return to school part-time to pursue a mechanical engineering degree. He said,

> My reasons for returning to school to pursue an engineering degree were that engineers got to work on a lot more interesting projects than non-engineers. The challenge and opportunities that engineers had was by far the biggest draw for me.[5]

Previously, Beatty had received an undergraduate degree in natural resources. He combined that background with his mechanical engineering degree to work in environmental engineering. He currently works for a natural gas and electric company in Minnesota that offers its customers incentives for increasing energy efficiency, which in turn helps the environment by cutting the amount of fuel and energy used. Beatty's job as energy efficiency manager is to analyze and determine the amount of energy savings for various improvements to homes, including roof and window replacements.

What other interesting projects has Beatty worked on? He answered,

> I have worked at an active refinery, which had several feet of oil floating on groundwater which they had to clean up. I

have seen soil so contaminated that when you squeezed it oil dropped out.[6]

He has also helped arrange for the cleanup of contaminated river water from a steel mill that was discharging wastewater over a long period of time.

Beatty offers this advice for students who want to become environmental engineers:

Hard work and dedication can help an aspiring engineer overcome a lot of obstacles and compensate for a lack of natural ability [or] intuition. I had a professor tell me he was always surprised by how hard-working students that he didn't think could cut it would eventually emerge triumphant. I can personally attest to that.[7]

A SPILL OF CATASTROPHIC PROPORTIONS

On April 20, 2010, an explosion on the British Petroleum Deepwater Horizon drilling rig in the Gulf of Mexico killed 11 workers and seriously injured 17 more. Within a week, oil leaking from the wellhead had grown to a slick on the surface of the ocean water reaching 100 miles (161 km) across. The National Oceanic and Atmospheric Administration estimated that the well was losing 5,000 barrels (682 t), or 210,000 gallons, every day.[8] By the time the well had been capped, nearly 4.9 million barrels (668,213 t) of oil had spilled into the gulf, making it the largest recorded maritime oil spill in US history.[9] President Barack Obama declared it one of the worst environmental disasters of all time. Environmental engineers contributed to the cleanup of the oil spill.

In laboratories, environmental engineers may conduct tests on polluted water samples.

A DAY IN THE LIFE OF AN ENVIRONMENTAL ENGINEER

Since environmental engineers work on diverse projects and in a range of areas, many report that they don't have a typical day. Yet many also say that this variety is what keeps their work fresh and exciting.

Many types of environmental engineers do share some daily routines, however. A typical day might include spending time outdoors—for example, overseeing the installation of a system to clean contaminated land. Next, the engineer might go back to the office and work on a computer to design a water treatment method. Then later in the day, he or she might meet with team members or clients.

THE TOP FIVE QUESTIONS ABOUT BECOMING AN ENVIRONMENTAL ENGINEER

1. *Do I need to get a degree in environmental engineering?*
   To work as an environmental engineer, you do need a bachelor's of science degree in engineering. However, a person who earns a degree in mechanical or civil engineering can sometimes work as an environmental engineer.

2. *I love being outside. Is environmental engineering the job for me?*
   Being outdoors can be a significant part of being an environmental engineer. Even so, much work is performed in a laboratory, an office, and meetings.

3. *I am physically disabled, yet I love science and dream of a job that allows me to help the environment. Can I still become an environmental engineer?*
   Absolutely! Not all environmental engineers are required to wade into lakes or hike into forests. Some work solely in lab and office settings using samples and findings gathered by others.

4. *I want to make a difference in the environment, but I don't like science. What jobs might be available for me?*
   Many jobs involve caring for the planet that don't require an aptitude for science. You may want to

consider becoming a conservationist for a department of natural resources. You might also consider being an environmental activist or a

"I was always interested in natural systems as a kid. As I got older I became more interested in how our human-built systems affected the natural systems and vice versa. Drinking water, waste water, and storm water deal with exactly that and that is what I work in now."[10]

—Christopher Harrington, environmental engineer

volunteer for a local group that teaches how to apply environmentally friendly principles to everyday life.

5. *How can I learn more about environmental engineering jobs?*

The Web sites of universities and professional organizations are great resources for jobs that will help you learn about becoming an environmental engineer. In addition, you should talk to people in the field. Most professionals enjoy sharing their experiences with those interested in their work. Also check with professional associations. They usually have an education or outreach group to provide more information about what they do.

Having a curiosity about environmentally friendly technology is a good attribute for an environmental engineer.

WOULD YOU MAKE A GOOD ENVIRONMENTAL ENGINEER?

Do you have what it takes to be a good environmental engineer? Learn more about the basic skills and abilities that most environmental engineers possess.

PASSION FOR SCIENCE AND EARTH

Successful environmental engineers enjoy the sciences and usually have an aptitude for biology, chemistry, geography, and math. They also have a passion for the environment. Environmental engineers enjoy looking at the earth and assessing how humans impact it. They often want to make a difference in the world for humans, animals, and nature.

PROBLEM-SOLVING SKILLS

Successful environmental engineers must be detail oriented and have good analytical skills. They must also have the ability to problem solve. They may, for example, need to figure out how best to dispose of household waste or what new recycling methods can be put to use. Thinking both creatively and practically, these engineers have to balance the needs of humans with the potential costs to the environment.

SUMMER JOBS WITH THE EPA

Every summer, the EPA hires high school and college students to work in the field and perform research. Doing these jobs gives students the chance "to gain vital work experience while contributing to the mission of protecting human health and safeguarding the environment."[1] Working for the EPA also provides a great opportunity for an emerging environmental engineer to get his or her foot in the door.

CURIOSITY AND RESEARCH

Other important qualities for an environmental engineer to have are a curious mind and a desire to continually learn. As technological processes evolve and improve and as Earth's environment changes due to human impact, environmental engineers must adapt, as well. Many engineers are required to take continuing education courses to stay knowledgeable on current environmental issues, procedures, laws, and technologies.

Environmental engineers must also dig deep into problems to come up with proper solutions. This often requires a good amount of research. Consider, for example, air pollution. Automobile and factory exhaust contribute high amounts of air pollutants every day. Yet pulling all the vehicles off the roads isn't an option, and neither is shutting down all the factories. Environmental engineers research the issues further and apply their problem-solving skills to find workable solutions.

TEAMWORK AND PUBLIC SPEAKING

Because environmental engineers often collaborate as part of a team, they need to be able to work well with others. Also, these engineers may need to speak with people face-to-face to discuss solutions to waste problems or to instruct company personnel how to improve or apply technologies for pollution control. Being comfortable and confident speaking in public is necessary for many environmental engineers.

Members of an environmental club may plant gardens and participate in other activities focused on improving the environment.

CHECKLIST

Would you make a good environmental engineer? Use this checklist to decide if it would be a good career fit for you:

- Are you interested in the environment and how humans interact with it?

- Do you enjoy chemistry, biology, and math?

- Do you enjoy volunteering with community cleanups and similar projects?

- Are you concerned about pollution?

- Do you have good problem-solving and analytical skills?

- Would you enjoy working outdoors at least part of the time?

If you answered yes to most of these questions, considering a career as an environmental engineer might be a smart move for you. If you answered no to some of the questions, environmental engineering may still be a career path for you. You can develop certain skills over time. However, environmental engineers usually possess a passion for wanting to improve the quality of the environment.

HOW TO GET THERE

IN HIGH SCHOOL

In high school, take as many biology, chemistry, and math classes as possible. Taking these classes will also help you develop the skills needed to be successful in college. If your high school offers AP or honors courses, take them.

Remember, many environmental engineers are consultants and have to instruct clients on how to approach a project. You may want to consider taking speech or communication classes to become comfortable with public speaking.

"Environmental engineers now are employed in virtually all heavy industries and utility companies in the United States, in any aspect of public works construction and management, by the EPA and other federal agencies, and by the consulting firms used by these agencies. In addition, every state and most local governments have agencies dealing with air quality, water quality and water resource management, soil quality, forest and natural resource management, and agricultural management that employ environmental engineers."[2]

—P. Aarne Vesilind, J. Jeffrey Peirce, and Ruth F. Weiner, Environmental Engineering

Extracurricular activities can help you prepare, too. Does your school have a green club? If so, join it. Members of these clubs participate in projects such as recycling and community education. Participating in such a club will help you start to understand environmental issues and gain focus for your career.

COLLEGE EDUCATION

Environmental engineers need to earn at least a bachelor's degree. Environmental engineering is a specialized form of

PROTECTING A LEGACY

Gabe Lee is an environmental engineer for Iowa's department of natural resources, which helps protect the state's waterways. "I always look at my job as protecting the interests of Iowa, for the people of Iowa," Lee said. "I'm trying to protect the streams and waterways in Iowa for them and for the children. That, I believe, is my legacy." [3]

civil engineering and frequently is part of the civil engineering program in colleges and universities. Some universities require students to earn a bachelor's degree in civil, mechanical, or chemical engineering and then supplement it with a minor in environmental engineering. Earning a bachelor's degree in environmental engineering can take five years at some universities.

Having a master's degree in environmental engineering can open up more job possibilities. Earning this degree can take two or three years. Having a PhD is recommended for those who wish to address global warming and other complex environmental issues. Pursuing a PhD will take another two to four years.

As with any engineering degree, environmental engineering requires taking courses that are challenging and demanding. Students must take advanced math, chemistry, and biology courses before beginning engineering courses. Some of the other required coursework might include statistics, environmental and sustainable engineering principles, environmental process engineering, introduction to groundwater hydrology, environmental systems and processes, and soil dynamics. Expect to take laboratory classes, as well.

GAIN EXPERIENCE

Many colleges have environmental engineering clubs or societies for students. These organizations provide excellent opportunities to meet people with interests similar to yours and to participate in field trips, competitions, and activities involving environmental engineering. Some of these organizations get involved in public service to help clean up communities.

Participating in clubs, organizations, and projects also shows employers your ongoing interest in and commitment to the field. And participation helps you network with people who might be able to assist you after graduation in finding a job, a graduate program, or a research opportunity.

ENGINEERING FOR WOMEN AND MINORITIES

Women and minorities have been underrepresented in the field of environmental engineering. To help more of these individuals earn degrees, several colleges and universities offer scholarships to women and minorities who choose to pursue environmental engineering. These schools also offer mentoring and other services to promote students' success in their programs. This educational support—coupled with the positive job outlook for engineers in this area—may result in more female and minority students becoming environmental engineers.

INTERNSHIP

Many engineering programs advise students to complete an internship. Being an intern allows a student to gain practical experience working under the supervision of an environmental engineer. As interns, students have the opportunity to apply their skills and knowledge while learning from experienced professionals. Employers who provide internships often offer jobs to successful interns and provide references for those who go on to graduate programs.

LICENSURE

In addition to receiving a degree, you should become a licensed professional engineer, as only licensed engineers are allowed to offer services to the public. Becoming licensed typically requires receiving a bachelor's degree and successfully completing two state exams. It may also involve a certain amount of work experience.

NETWORKING

Since environmental engineers often work as consultants, becoming well known in the profession is important. Meeting and mingling with others in the profession is an important step in gaining clients. You will also stand a better chance of successfully collaborating with other engineers if you get to know them. And if you are looking for a full-time job with a company, you will have a much better chance at getting an interview if you know someone there who is aware of your enthusiasm, interest, and commitment to doing excellent work. Having a personal connection will help you avoid being treated as just another résumé in the pile.

Consulting on projects is a great way for an environmental engineer to network.

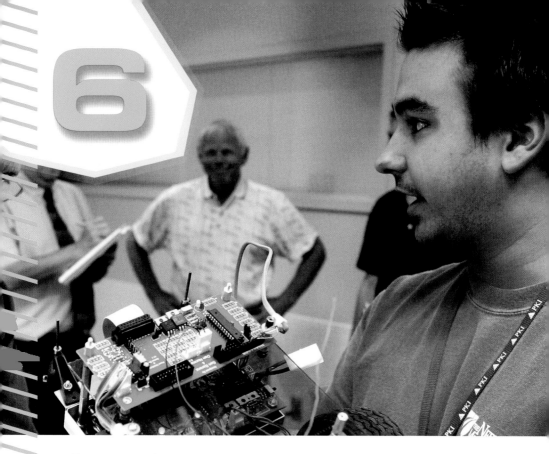

Computer engineers work on new and exciting technology, including robots that can be used to teach math and science to kids.

WHAT IS A COMPUTER ENGINEER?

Computer engineers design, develop, test, and implement computer-based hardware and software. They construct the computer systems and components that go into countless objects, products, and services. The men and women who do this work are the brains behind the processors and circuitry that make everyday life easier, happier, and healthier. Computer engineers research and use critical-thinking skills to create cool technological inventions, such as MP3 players and personal digital assistants.

Computer engineers generally specialize in hardware or software. Computer hardware refers to the physical parts of the computer: the hard drive, the display or monitor, the keyboard, and the microchips and circuits inside the machine. Computer software refers to the programs and data that tell the computer what to do. When you open up a computer application that allows you to type a letter or create a spreadsheet, you are using the computer's software. Software can include such things as computer games, business applications, operating systems, and network control systems.

Computer software engineers devise ways to put computers to work. They create, test, and evaluate software applications using computer science

FROM FILM TO PIXELS

Thanks to the inventive minds of computer engineers, snapping pictures of moments you want to remember is much easier—and less expensive—than it once was. Computer architects and engineers developed the digital imaging equipment that underlies today's digital cameras. No longer dependent on film, digital cameras can store hundreds of pictures on a single memory card and allow the photographer to view the image immediately after it's captured.

principles and mathematics. Some computer engineers develop new microprocessors, which house the central processing unit (CPU) of the computer. The CPU is the element that carries out a computer's functions. Other computer engineers design operating systems, which are software programs that allow communication between the hardware and other software applications. Without an operating system, such as Microsoft Windows or Mac OS X, you would not be able to use your software, and therefore, you would not get much use out of your computer.

Computer engineers are often involved in creating supercomputers. These are ultrafast computers, capable of computing and calculating large, complex amounts of data instantaneously. Supercomputers are often used for forecasting the weather, making astrophysics computations, predicting earthquakes, or performing any scientific activities that require large amounts of calculations. Some computer engineers help install and

COMPUTER AND ELECTRICAL ENGINEERS

Computer engineers and electrical engineers sometimes work collaboratively on electronics technology. Both also oversee production of computer and electronic components and equipment. "It's a rewarding feeling to look out onto a factory floor and see product that you designed and developed by working with software and mechanical engineers being built," said Jonathan Mueller, an electrical engineer.[1]

Some computer engineers spend most of their days on computers.

monitor supercomputers in research centers and other facilities.

Robotics is another area that computer engineers may choose to pursue. They help design motors and sensors for industrial robots that perform specific tasks, such as welding in automobile manufacturing. Computer engineers also contribute to aerospace, medicine, pharmaceuticals, automotives, and communications. They create software systems that secure the nation's power grid, ensure data privacy, and enable communications and media.

WHAT IS A COMPUTER ENGINEER'S WORK ENVIRONMENT?

Depending on the type of job a computer engineer has, his or her daily work setting can differ. Many computer engineers work in offices or from remote work sites, which can be any place with a computer and Internet access.

Some engineers sit at a computer all day long, helping design new operating systems. Others work on integrating computers into space shuttles, airplanes, and other high-tech vehicles. Some work with small consumer electronics, while others collaborate to develop large-scale computerized manufacturing tools. As a computer engineer, you might find yourself in a state-of-the-art lab, working with a large group of engineers, or you might work at a smaller company, implementing new computer systems for staff.

WHAT IS THE JOB MARKET FOR COMPUTER ENGINEERS?

As of May 2008, approximately 514,800 computer software engineers were employed in the United States.[2] And the United States employed 74,700 computer hardware engineers.[3] On average, the median annual wage for software engineers was $85,430.[4] Hardware engineers' median wage was $97,400.[5]

The US Department of Labor projects that by 2018, the number of software engineers will rise to 689,900.[6] And the number of hardware engineers will rise to 77,500.[7] This represents a 34 percent increase in software engineer positions.[8] This is a 4 percent increase in hardware engineer positions.[9]

PROFILE OF A COMPUTER ENGINEER

When Jourdan Bennett was in fourth grade, he began writing simple computer programs for fun. In sixth grade, he joined the technology club at his grade school, which introduced him to more complicated programming. With the support of his father—a math teacher who taught him shortcuts to make math fun and entertaining—Bennett was well on his way to becoming a computer engineer.

Bennett said he more or less fell into the field of software engineering. In college, he received a bachelor's of science degree in marketing with a minor in computer science. After graduating, he was hired by a consulting company that was looking for

COMPUTERS ARE EVERYWHERE

Try to remember the last time you went an entire day without using some form of computer technology. It's difficult to do! If you bought things at a store where a clerk scanned your items, heated up your lunch in a microwave, used a cell phone, or washed clothes in the washing machine, you came into contact with computers. Did you know your car has a computer? If your bathroom scale has a digital readout, it, too, has a computer. Computer engineers are the geniuses behind all of the computerized items we use on a daily basis.

candidates with business degrees. The company wanted staff that understood the business world and could also apply computer programming skills. After starting the job, Bennett had 13 weeks of intensive training to learn a computer programming language.

Bennett's first work in the computer field was updating mainframe computers to head off the much-anticipated problems prior to January 1, 2000. At the time, many computers were not able to handle the changeover from the two-digit year of '99 to '00. After the Y2K scare ended, Bennett received additional training to learn the fundamentals of software quality assurance engineering.

Bennett explained, "My current job position is software test engineer. I am responsible for verifying the functionality, robustness, reliability, and performance of software incorporated into our [company's] products."[10] In this position, Bennett works on a project that archives video recorded from cameras located all around the United States to DVDs or Blu-ray discs for long-term storage. One of the uses for

NOT YOUR GRANDMOTHER'S FRIDGE

In 2007, LG Electronics released the first digital, high-definition television refrigerator. In addition to having a digitally programmable ice maker, this appliance offers a 15-inch (38 cm), high-definition television screen with DVD capabilities, plus a 4-inch (10 cm) LCD display that provides personalized weather forecasts. Other perks include an FM radio, a digital photo album display, and 100 recipes preloaded into the refrigerator's computer.

the stored video data will be for evidence in courts of law. Bennett's job is to make sure the software meets the client's requirements.

Bennett spends a typical day at the office mainly at his computer, running through tests of software. Any problem he finds requires him to write up a defect report. He passes that report on to the developer, who is responsible for fixing the problem. Bennett then retests the software and verifies the developer has solved the problem. Bennett says,

> I work very closely with the other software test engineers and the software engineers at my company. I enjoy being able to work as a team member responsible for the overall quality of our software and having the responsibility of my own individual task; it's the best of both worlds.[11]

A DAY IN THE LIFE OF A COMPUTER ENGINEER

What can you expect of a typical day as a computer engineer? The possibilities are as diverse as the jobs, so it depends mainly on what area a computer engineer works in. Still, most computer engineers spend a good deal of time at a computer. Whether they are working to develop software or diagramming a new hardware concept, computer use is certain. Most computer engineers can expect to work a regular 40-hour week. However, their work environment allows for flexibility, so some engineers work remotely.

Teamwork is a big part of computer engineering. These engineers collaborate with other computer engineers and with electrical and mechanical engineers to join different engineering principles for achieving a common goal. For example, to create the next great roller coaster, structural, mechanical, electrical, and computer engineers work together to design, build, and implement the ride.

Computer engineers design smart phones and their applications.

TOP FIVE QUESTIONS ABOUT BECOMING A COMPUTER ENGINEER

1. *As a computer engineer, will I spend my entire day in front of a computer?*

   Most jobs in computer engineering involve a lot of computer work but some hands-on work as well. For instance, computer engineers may work with the components of computers. Most jobs also require team interaction and meetings with coworkers and clients.

2. *I love technology! Is computer engineering the right career for me?*

   A passion for technology will certainly assist you in this career path. Computers are constantly evolving, so enjoying learning about the latest computers, software, and technology will help you reach your goal. Electrical engineering may be a route for you to explore, too.

3. *What are some good ways of learning about computers and electronics?*

   Use technology! That's probably the best way to learn about computers and electronics. Use new programs, and think about what you do and don't like about them and why. What would you do to make the program better? Reading is another great way to soak up information. Countless online articles are available about computers, electronics, and technology. You can also subscribe to a number of magazines dedicated to these topics.

4. *Must I have a degree in computer engineering to work in the field?*

To work as a computer engineer, you will most likely need a bachelor's degree in engineering. However, sometimes someone with a degree in a similar or related field, such as electrical engineering, can work as a computer engineer, depending on the job requirements.

5. *What is a cool project that I might work on as a computer engineer?*

A decade ago, most cell phones could only make and receive phone calls. Screens didn't have color, and ringer options were very limited. Today, smart phones allow users not only to customize their own ringtones but also to take and send pictures, surf the Internet, send e-mails, store and play digital music, and use countless applications—all on a big, bright, touch screen. These phones were created by specialized computer engineers called computer architects, who devise ways to make computers both smaller and more efficient.

Some computer engineers are good at troubleshooting hardware problems.

WOULD YOU MAKE A GOOD COMPUTER ENGINEER?

A re you thinking that becoming a computer engineer might be for you? Are you wondering if you have what it takes to be successful in this line of work? Here's your chance to do some self-assessment. Most computer engineers have a specific set of personal qualities and skills.

COMPUTER AND MATH SKILLS

Many computer engineers remember enjoying a variety of science and computer classes when they were young. They loved learning about how things worked and often enjoyed taking apart and rebuilding things—especially computer hard drives and electronics.

Whether designing the next great supercomputer or developing new software, computer engineers must have a deep, clear understanding of computers. They must also be able to learn and apply computer languages, such as C++ and JavaScript.

Computer engineers have a gift for math, including

THE FIRST COMPUTER PROGRAM

Although the computer has been a household item for only the last few decades, the first computer program dates back to 1843. August Ada Byron, daughter of famous English poet Lord Byron, was a gifted mathematician. She studied the works of Englishman Charles Babbage, including his difference engine, which was a very early form of the modern-day calculator. Byron then went on to translate and add notes to an article about Babbage's analytical engine that was written in Italian. In her notes, she explained how the analytical engine could be programmed to calculate certain numbers.

Byron's explanation is considered the first computer program. To honor her accomplishment, in 1979, a computer programming language called Ada was named for her.

BARBIE BECOMES A COMPUTER ENGINEER

In early 2010, the Mattel toy company conducted a worldwide online vote in which people helped choose the first in a new line of career-inspired Barbie dolls. The results of the vote were announced in February 2010: fans had chosen Computer Engineer Barbie. For her new role as a computer engineer, the popular doll received a makeover. She was outfitted with a pink laptop, pink glasses, trendy tennis shoes, a tech-inspired T-shirt, and a smart phone. Although Computer Engineer Barbie was the 126th career-inspired doll, she was the first doll whose career was chosen by consumers.

Excited about the positive influence the new Computer Engineer Barbie may have on young science-minded girls, Nora Lin, the president of the Society of Women Engineers, commented, "As a computer engineer, Barbie will show girls that women can turn their ideas into realities that have a direct and positive impact on people's everyday lives in this exciting and rewarding career."[1]

algebra, trigonometry, and calculus. They are also good at creating algorithms, which are methods for solving problems using sequences of instructions. Algorithms are used to perform mathematical calculations and to perform complex sorting and searching of data. Learning algorithms is an upper-level task, but having a passion for math can help a budding computer engineer reach this goal.

COMMUNICATION SKILLS

Computer engineers work closely with programmers, designers, product developers, and testers. To do so, these engineers need to have strong interpersonal and communication skills, as well as the ability to work in a team. To discuss a project with other members of the team or to meet with customers and clients, computer engineers must be able to communicate effectively with both their fellow engineers and people unfamiliar with computer terminology.

ABILITY TO TROUBLESHOOT

Much of what computer engineers do on a daily basis is troubleshooting: applying their knowledge of computer systems and hardware to solve problems. If a computer crashes or malfunctions, computer engineers must use their critical-thinking and computer skills to provide a solution.

ENJOYING A FAST-PACED INDUSTRY

Computers and technology change rapidly, and computer engineers must keep up. To do so, engineers must be forward thinking and innovative. Most engineers enjoy learning about the latest and greatest trends and technological advancements. They also get excited about inventing new things and finding new ways to integrate computers into everyday life.

PATIENCE AND DETERMINATION

Computer engineers do quite a bit of testing—followed by even more testing. They must work through a new product's bugs and glitches before arriving at the finished version.

During an internship, an intern works with other computer engineers, making connections in the industry.

Trying to pinpoint and then fix each problem can be tedious and frustrating. Computer engineers must also test computer components and devices to ensure they meet specifications. Performing these tests requires patience, determination, and great attention to detail.

CHECKLIST

Are you a good candidate for a career in computer engineering? Use this checklist to help you decide if you have the right skills and attributes:

- *Are you good at problem solving?*

- *Do you have excellent computer and math skills?*

- *Do you like thinking of ways to automate tasks?*

- *When you fail at something, do you regroup and try again?*

- *Do you like using existing tools to develop new ideas and real-world applications?*

- *Are you the type of person who pays attention to small details?*

- *Are you excited to learn and use new computer applications?*

If you answered yes to most of these questions, you might have the skills needed to become a computer engineer. If you lack some of these skills right now, that doesn't mean you should rule out computer engineering altogether. Going to college will provide you with the necessary classes you need. You will also have time to further develop your computer abilities and personal skills.

HOW TO GET THERE

IN HIGH SCHOOL

Take as many computer classes as your high school offers. Taking advanced math classes, such as trigonometry and calculus, will help you, as well. Does your school have honors or AP classes? Take them. Taking challenging courses will not only help you get into a good university, but it will prepare you for more difficult coursework.

Join an organization such as the Junior Engineering Technical Society (JETS), which sponsors academic competitions. The knowledge you will gain from participating in competitions will give you an extra boost in preparing for college. In addition, organizations such as JETS sometimes offer college scholarships.

Jump in early and learn some programming languages, such as C++, Java, and XML. Also talk with people in the field. Ask them for tips and advice. Find out whether their companies allow high school students to job shadow. Spending a

RANKING ENGINEERING PROGRAMS

Every year, *U.S. News & World Report* issues a list of the top-ranking US universities with engineering programs. The ranking is based on evaluations that include peer assessment, recruiter assessment, and research activity. In 2009, MIT was ranked the number-one graduate school for computer engineering. In 2010, MIT was ranked the top school overall for engineering. Stanford University in Stanford, California, came in second.[2]

day at work with a computer engineer will give you the best idea of what he or she does on the job.

COLLEGE EDUCATION

A computer engineer must have at least a bachelor's degree in computer engineering, computer programming, or software engineering. Earning this degree can take four or five years, depending on the requirements of the university and the program. Some students continue on to earn a master's degree or a PhD, each of which can take another two or three years.

Computer engineering courses are heavy in topics such as computer science, math, programming, electronics, and circuits. Advanced math classes include calculus and equations. Typically, the student must complete calculus classes before beginning core classes in computer engineering. The student must also

COMPUTER ENGINEERS IN HOLLYWOOD

Are you passionate about computers and movies? Why not work with both? Computer software engineers have developed and designed computer graphic (CG) animation software, including programs for lighting, shading, texturing, and other three-dimensional elements of computer-assisted animation design. These programs have been used by animation artists to bring to life movies such as *Toy Story, Happy Feet, Cars,* and *Legends of the Guardians: The Owls of Ga'Hoole.* The Harry Potter movies, as well as *The Chronicles of Narnia,* have also relied on CG software to produce special effects.

take certain courses to specialize in software or hardware engineering.

INTERNSHIPS

After completing your college courses or during your senior year, it is advised to do an internship. As an intern, you will work for computer engineers and receive training in a real work setting. Although the pay for an internship is often lower than that for an entry-level career position, the experience will be well worth it. You will be learning from experienced professionals and given the chance to demonstrate your skills and abilities by working on projects. In some cases, an internship may lead to a job offer from the internship employer. Regardless, all internships provide a starting point for getting hired into a career position.

A computer engineer may design a robot that collects scientific data in icy environments.

Video game developers work in relaxed atmospheres and play their games to test them.

WHAT IS A VIDEO GAME DEVELOPER?

Simply put, video game developers create video games. However, the development process requires a team effort and involves input from many different professionals with creativity, ingenuity, and engineering skills.

Typically, a game designer is part of the game development team and has the clearest vision of where the project is headed. He or she acts as a creative leader and is responsible for the outcome of the finished game. The game designer may be a programmer, or he or she might be a member of the artistic team or another group working on the game project.

Once the project and vision have been clearly set, the next step is to bring in writers. They are responsible for detailing the story line of the game. They also need to write any tutorials that may instruct the game's users in how to maneuver through it.

Next, programmers work on computer code to design the game. Many times, they are computer software engineers. These programmers develop the game's source code, which is the collection of statements written in a computer programming language that specify the actions to be performed by the computer and video game console. The code allows the game to work as intended.

Once the programmers have determined the game's source code, artists are brought in to create the terrain, landscape, characters, and other objects in the game world. Artists and other developers sketch a rough design of the game world, often creating a storyboard. A storyboard is a series of drawings that show the progression of actions or the sequence of levels in the game. Creating a storyboard allows the team to visualize the game. Some video game artists are talented individuals who use their computer engineering degrees in an artistic way.

VIDEO GAMES— SOMETHING FOR EVERYONE

Do you think playing video games is just for kids? Think again. According to a 2010 report by the Entertainment Software Association, 67 percent of all Americans play computer and video games. The average age of players is 34 years old. Forty-nine percent of players are between the ages of 18 and 49, and more than one-quarter are over the age of 50. Sixty-seven percent of all US homes have either a game console or a computer that's used to play games.[1]

Programmers then use game development software to create graphics of the artists' design and to implement command systems for game tasks—for example, integrating sound effects, simulating object movements, and providing other important pieces of the video game puzzle. A video game designer may decide the game will include a racetrack or road and a variety of cars will race upon it. The programmer then has the job of creating code that will dictate the speed of the cars, how they will swerve around obstacles, and how they will crash. Programmers also have the job of ensuring the game operates smoothly.

The music and sounds of the game are the responsibility of musicians and sound designers. Testers are involved as well to make sure the game is free of bugs or glitches. All of these people have their own expertise but work together to create a video game.

WHAT IS A VIDEO GAME DEVELOPER'S WORK ENVIRONMENT?

Video game developers typically work in an office, where they collaborate closely with other members of the design team. While video game developing is detail-oriented work that requires organization, responsibility, and commitment, the office setting is typically more relaxed than most other business environments. For instance, video game developers aren't usually expected to wear formal business attire to work every day. Some game companies even have areas where employees can spend time unwinding, such as a lounge with a table tennis or foosball table.

However, being a video game developer isn't all fun and games. At times, developers work under high pressure and stress. Whether they work for a large company that produces its own games or a small company that designs games for

> "There are games now for pretty much every age, every demographic. More and more women are going online. It comes down to everybody is playing games. Games are just evolving like species in order to fit into every little niche of our lives."[2]
>
> —*Jesse Schell, instructor of entertainment technology at Carnegie Mellon University*

a video game publisher, they have deadlines to meet. This might mean working late nights or weekends. Because of the

Attending game developing conferences is important to a video game developer's job.

demands of this work, a high level of burnout is sometimes associated with video game developers.

WHAT IS THE JOB MARKET FOR VIDEO GAME DEVELOPERS?

In 2008, *Game Developer Magazine,* a leading publication in the video game industry, reported that the average income for a game developer in the United States was $77,010.[3] In 2008, nearly 209,000 people in the United States were employed in the video game industry as designers.[4]

Breaking into the video game industry can be tough. It's a competitive profession, and usually only the best designers and developers become successful. However, sales of video games continue to grow. The outlook for the field over the next few years is positive for those who have the determination to work through the busy times and put in the long hours.

A PROFILE OF A VIDEO GAME DEVELOPER

Brian Colin is a funny, friendly man who has been designing and developing video games for nearly 30 years. After completing his college coursework for a major in film production at Southern Illinois University, he spent about a year and a half, as he explained, "knocking around sort of as a roving cartoonist" and living on very little money.[5] One day, he answered an ad for a video game company in Illinois that was looking for a video artist.

Looking back, Colin admitted the level of art used in early video games was rather simple compared to what's used today. At first, he was a bit apprehensive about how interesting the job would be, but he was lured by the promise of a steady paycheck and benefits. Laughing, he said, "I remember thinking as I hung up the phone, 'This is it. Childhood is officially over. I've got a real job.' Ah, I was wrong!"[6]

Colin started his new job with a head full of artistic ideas and a creative imagination. He got to work helping design art for arcade games, which became the start of his career in video game design. He codeveloped several hit games, including Rampage, a successful arcade game from 1985. He also set new standards with innovative games such as Pigskin 621 AD and Arch Rivals. The starving artist had found a lucrative niche.

In 1992, Colin and fellow designer Jeff Nauman left the company they had been working for to form their own video game company, Game Refuge. Today, in their office in Homewood, Illinois, they employ a team of designers and developers who have helped them create best-selling video games such as Rampage World Tour and Star Trek Voyager. Since beginning their partnership, Colin and Nauman have designed and developed more than 60 games, including arcade games, casino

ONLINE PLAY

Richard Garriott is one of the world's most famous game designers. From 1979 to 1980, he worked on Akalabeth and Ultima I, both role-playing video games for home computers. His first commercially successful game, Akalabeth, was based on a game he designed while still in high school. He sold the game to a game publisher when he was just 19 years old. Both Akalabeth and Ultima I, which feature swords-and-sorcery fantasy worlds, became wildly popular. They are still considered groundbreaking works of video game design.

By the mid-1990s, Garriott was again on the verge of breaking new ground in the world of gaming. With the advent of the computer modem and easy access to the Internet, he wondered if players from all over could play a single game online. Garriott used the idea to develop Ultima Online, the first massively multiplayer game. Ultima Online was the first game in the multibillion-dollar online game industry.

slot games, and touch screen games.

The story of Colin's career demonstrates that video game developers can come from all walks of life. In hiring his own staff, he says he doesn't necessarily look for people with degrees in video game design. "I try to hire well-rounded individuals; I look for talent and attitude rather than specific skill sets. I figure I can always teach a talented person a new tool," he explained.[7]

> ## COMING TO A THEATER NEAR YOU
>
> Have you ever heard of Lara Croft? How about Mario and Luigi? Are you familiar with a place called Raccoon City? Video games have become so prominent that sometimes their characters become part of culture. Many action-packed characters have sprung to life on the silver screen in the form of hugely anticipated movies, such as *Tomb Raider, Resident Evil,* and *Mortal Kombat.* Some of these films have become multimillion-dollar blockbusters.

A DAY IN THE LIFE OF A VIDEO GAME DEVELOPER

If you choose a career in video game development, you can expect to spend your time in a variety of ways. According to Colin,

No two days are ever the same. Some days are filled with blue-sky invention and group brainstorming sessions frantically scribbling on a whiteboard as ideas by the dozens

are tossed out for consideration. Other days are spent in solitary seclusion as you push a few stray pixels ever closer to perfection.[8]

Still, most video game developers work a great deal on a computer, programming, writing, planning, or using special software to draw and design game characters and settings.

Some of a video game developer's time is dedicated to brainstorming new game ideas, writing computer code that allows the games to play as expected, troubleshooting likely problems, and communicating and collaborating with other team members. Most game developers also attend trade shows and conventions, which help them stay current on the latest trends and expectations in video games.

Developers also find themselves in front of the games, playing them. Whether testing a prototype game, looking for game bugs, or keeping up their skills, playing video games is all part of a day's work for video game developers.

Shigeru Miyamoto, a video game designer for Nintendo,
demonstrates a game for an audience.

TOP FIVE QUESTIONS ABOUT BECOMING A VIDEO GAME DEVELOPER

1. *Do I need to be good at playing video games to become a video game developer?*

    While many people in the video game industry enjoy playing video games and got into the business because of their love for games, plenty of others don't play video games in their spare time. Artists, writers, and engineers can be drawn to video game development because of their love for creating art, stories, and programs—not necessarily because they are skilled or dedicated players.

2. *I don't know computer programming, and I'm not a great artist. Can I still consider video game development as a career?*

    Video game design companies look for people with imagination, enthusiasm, and diverse real-world interests. Do you have fresh ideas? Do you like to work collaboratively on projects? Designing video games requires more than artists and computer programmers, so don't give up on your dream. But do be prepared to state what your dream is and demonstrate that you are able to learn the skills the job requires.

3. *Who's in charge of thinking up new video games?*
   Any member of the development team can come up
   with a game idea. Then after the initial idea has been
   put in place, the project becomes a collaborative effort
   to make that vision a reality. Each team member then
   performs his or her role in the game development.

4. *I've come up with some of my own game ideas and
   designs. Should I show them to an employer if I get
   an interview?*
   Employers like to see you are willing to try things on
   your own. It shows you are eager and self-motivated.
   In addition, employers like to hear what games you do
   and don't like and why. The why is the important part
   because employers want to see the thought process
   behind your opinion.

5. *If I become a video game developer, will I get to sit around
   all day and play games?*
   While testing games and checking for bugs might
   be part of your job, it won't take up most of your
   workday. You will also work on designs, meet with
   other developers, brainstorm, and accomplish many
   other tasks involved in game development.

People who have a passion for playing video games may find video game developing to be a career path for them.

WOULD YOU MAKE A GOOD VIDEO GAME DEVELOPER?

D oes a career as a video game developer sound appealing to you? Many developers say they love their jobs. If you have the drive to learn and the ability to keep an open mind and offer ideas on a regular basis, you might have what it takes to be a successful video game developer. Learn more about some of the main traits and skills video game developers possess.

IMAGINATION

Designing video games requires a great deal of imagination. Coming up with ideas for games and then turning them into fun and challenging games requires developers to think very creatively.

COMMUNICATION AND ORGANIZATIONAL SKILLS

Writing and communication skills are essential in the video game world. Developers need to be able to bounce ideas off one another. They must also be able to communicate suggestions for changes to designers, including their reasons for the changes. Developers often work on more than one project at a time. They need to have good organizational skills to keep track of separate assignments and deadlines.

"People are beginning to understand it really is a career. This is a growth industry, a big growth industry. And I think we are going to see wonderful things happen that we haven't even imagined yet."[1]

—Elizabeth Daley, dean of the University of Southern California School of Cinematic Arts, of a career in video game design

College students may learn how to program games
in a gaming lab.

WORKING WELL UNDER PRESSURE

To meet deadlines, developers must be able to work long hours and under pressure. "If you want to work nine to five, this is the wrong industry," warns David Riley of the NPD Group. "Deadlines are fierce."[2]

COMPUTERS AND TRENDS

Excellent computer skills are required of game developers. Most spend hours each day working on a computer, doing any of several tasks: programming, using graphic design software to draw, writing story lines, or detailing the game's blueprint.

Developers must also keep up with evolving trends in the game industry. Game concepts change over time, as do technology and user expectations.

CHECKLIST

Do you have the makings of a video game developer? Answer the questions below to find out:

- *Do you enjoy entertaining people?*

- *Do you like video games?*

- *Are you willing to work long hours and do what's necessary to get the job done?*

- *Do you work well with others on a team?*

- *Are you an imaginative person?*

- *Are you willing to learn skills and try new things?*

- *Do you work well with deadlines?*

- *Are you a good communicator?*

If your answer was yes to most of these questions, you might make a great video game developer. Are you thinking to yourself, "What if I answered no to most of these questions?" Don't panic. If you have the determination to learn and the willingness to try, you still have time to develop some of these skills and try your hand at becoming a video game developer.

HOW TO GET THERE

IN HIGH SCHOOL

While still in high school, start acquiring some of the skills needed to become a video game developer. Although you don't necessarily have to be a good artist to be a developer, if you enjoy art and have a talent for it, take as many art classes as possible. Also take all the math and computer classes you can. Computer concepts classes—especially scripting and graphic design classes—will be especially useful.

Take advantage of English and communications classes, too. Become comfortable speaking to people, whether in a group setting or

DESIGN DOCUMENT

Communication is key for video game developers. To have a clear understanding of a new game in development, developers draft a design document. The team refers to this for the description of the game, an outline of the basic concept of game play, and an in-depth account of the technical aspects of the game, such as characters, levels, and a description of the graphics and style of the art. Using the design document allows every team member to be on the same page and to understand the mission of the game design. The design document answers the following questions:

- What is the game hero's goal?
- What skills or powers does he/she/it have?
- How many enemies or obstacles must the hero face?
- How many players can play at once?
- What is the game player's perspective: side view, top view, or first person?

one-on-one. You may find yourself having to pitch a game idea to a potential publisher, and you will want to sound confident and knowledgeable.

What can you do in addition to taking classes? Play video games, of course. Familiarize yourself with a wide variety of games and game genres. Action, adventure, first-person shooter, simulations, role-playing—give them all a try. Playing games will sharpen your problem-solving skills, as well as introduce you to an assortment of game concepts.

> "I encourage everyone to go away to college, if possible, if for no other reason than to simply enjoy a prolonged childhood. Truth is, four years of simply 'figuring things out' is exactly the kind of broad, problem-solving experience that one needs to be a designer."[4]
>
> —Brian Colin, video game designer and CEO of Game Refuge

Colin encourages students to dive into game design. "There are hundreds of free and/or inexpensive game creation tools and forums on the Internet," he says. "The sooner you start, the further you'll go."[3]

COLLEGE

To date, more than 200 US colleges, universities, and technical schools offer programs for video game design and development. In these programs, you will take classes that teach animation, gaming technology, and game design process.

GAIN EXPERIENCE

Several video game design companies offer internships that allow for real-world work experience as part of a video game design team. Another way to gain experience in the field is to get a job as a video game tester. Although different from a video game developer, the position of video game tester will allow you to learn more about the industry and perhaps get your foot in the door at a design company.

Being self-motivated is important in the video game developing world. To get more experience, try designing your own video game or adding new levels to an existing game. These projects can become part of your portfolio, the collection of work you show to potential employers.

A TRUE RATE OF PAY

Video game developers average $77,010 a year in salary.[5] While this seems like a lot of money, it comes at a cost. Most developers don't receive overtime pay. This means they might work long, hard hours for weeks or months on end to meet a deadline and receive no extra compensation. In a 2007 article on MSNBC.com, Christine Miller, a Seattle-based video game designer, commented about the then-current median salary of video game developers: "$73,000 sounds great until you realize you've just spent 6 months or more working 80 hour weeks, your friends forgot who you are and you haven't seen your new niece or nephew yet." However, she added, "But I can't picture doing anything else."[6]

An internship at a video game company could help you
break into the industry.

GET YOUR FOOT IN THE DOOR

Considering what career to pursue is a huge personal decision. To become an engineer, you will need to earn a college degree, which requires personal commitment, dedication, and determination. Also, the more you know about the profession you intend to go into, the better prepared you will be to achieve your goal.

There's no better way to start preparing than to get involved in the profession now. Hunt for a part-time job that introduces you to some of the tasks involved in engineering or video game development. Look into doing an internship at an engineering company or being a video game tester. Doing so will give you a glimpse into the profession and give you a feel for what personal skills and qualities you will need to succeed.

Many people are willing and eager to share advice and information about their line of work. Talk to your career counselor for information on how to contact people in the engineering or video game industry. Ask them if you can arrange to job shadow, accompanying them to work to see and experience what their daily responsibilities include. Job shadowing is a wonderful opportunity to see firsthand what the profession is all about. If job shadowing isn't possible, conducting an informational interview can be a great way to gain insight into a career. An informational interview is conducted to get advice about a career, rather than to get a job. Informational interviews can be done in person, over the telephone, or through e-mail.

Whether you are looking for a part-time job or an internship, be prepared for the interview process. Practice answering potential interview questions with a friend or your parents. To come up with sample interview questions, ask someone currently working in the field. He or she may also be able to offer other helpful tips on what to expect during an interview. Online resources are also available that can help you practice phone and in-person interviews.

The most important thing is that you stay proactive. *You* are the one who can decide your future path and take the necessary steps to get there. Stay focused and informed. Read, research, ask questions, and become involved. The more experience you gain now, the better your chance of getting your foot in the door for your future career.

PROFESSIONAL ORGANIZATIONS

Here are some professional organizations that might be able to help you with more information on the jobs covered in this book.

CHEMICAL ENGINEER

American Chemical Society
www.acs.org

American Institute of Chemical Engineers
http://www.aiche.org

Association of Energy Engineers
www.aeecenter.org

Electrochemical Society
www.electrochem.org

Society of Women Engineers
http://societyofwomenengineers.swe.org

ENVIRONMENTAL ENGINEER

American Academy of Environmental Engineers
www.aaee.net

American Society of Professional Wetland Engineers
http://aspwe.org

Association of Environmental Engineering and Science
Professors
www.aeesp.org

COMPUTER ENGINEER

Association for Computing Machinery
www.acm.org

Computing Research Association
http://cra.org

IEEE Computer Society
www.computer.org

VIDEO GAME DEVELOPER

Entertainment Software Association
www.theesa.com

Georgia Game Developers Association
www.ggda.org

International Game Developers Association
www.igda.org

MARKET FACTS

JOB	NUMBER OF JOBS	GROWTH RATE	
Chemical Engineer	31,700	little or no change	
Environmental Engineer	54,300	much faster than average	
Computer Software Engineer	514,800	much faster than average	
Computer Hardware Engineer	74,700	much slower than average	
Video Game Developer	209,000*	about as fast as average	

	MEDIAN WAGE	RELATED JOBS	SKILLS
	$84,680	biotechnologist, chemist, chemical technician	analytical, detail oriented, aptitude for math and science
	$74,020	civil engineer, environmental planner, global conservationist, DNR conservationist	passion for Earth, curious, good research skills
	$85,430	computer programmer, electrical engineer, computer technician	aptitude for math, computer skills, patience
	$97,400	computer programmer, electrical engineer, computer technician	aptitude for math, computer skills, patience
	$77,010*	graphic artist, video game tester	imaginative, team player, deadline oriented

* Statistics from O*NET OnLine
All other statistics from the *Bureau of Labor Statistics Occupational Outlook Handbook, 2010–2011 Edition*

GLOSSARY

aerospace
Earth's atmosphere and the space beyond it.

algorithm
A set of step-by-step procedures for solving a problem.

aqueduct
A structure built for carrying a large amount of flowing water.

astrophysics
A branch of astronomy concerned with the chemical and physical properties of celestial bodies.

ecosystem
An environment and its organisms that function as one unit.

engineering
The application of math and science to make products and processes that are useful to people.

hydrology
The science dealing with water and how it circulates on the ground and in the atmosphere.

microchip
A system of electronic components and connections housed on a tiny piece of silicon.

microprocessor
A component of a computer that executes the command to start booting up a computer and activates the necessary computer components, such as the operating system.

MP3

A computer file format for audio data, usually songs.

networking

Connecting with people and developing relationships that will impact business.

petrochemical

A chemical made from petroleum or natural gas.

polymer

A substance such as a plastic that is made up of a complex chain of molecules.

prototype

A full-scale, functional example of a new design.

quantum mechanics

The behavior of matter and energy at the atomic and subatomic levels.

refinery

The building and equipment where refining and processing of a product such as oil takes place.

supercomputer

A very fast computer that is used to calculate scientific computations.

ADDITIONAL RESOURCES

FURTHER READINGS

Adams, Ernest, *Break Into the Game Industry: How to Get a Job Making Video Games*. Emeryville, CA: McGraw, 2003. Print.

Cunningham, Kevin. *Video Game Designer*. Ann Arbor, MI: Cherry Lake, 2009. Print.

Hutson, Matt. *Cool Careers in Engineering*. San Diego, CA: Sally Ride Science, 2010. Print.

Levy, Matthys. *Engineering the City: How Infrastructure Works: Projects and Principles for Beginners*. Chicago: Chicago Review, 2000. Print.

McClelland, Carol L. *Green Careers for Dummies*. Hoboken, NJ: Wiley, 2010. Print.

McCoy, Lisa. *Career Launcher: Video Games*. New York: Ferguson, 2010. Print.

McDavid, Richard A. *Career Opportunities in Engineering*. New York: Ferguson, 2010. Print.

Reeves, Diane Lindsey. *Career Ideas for Kids Who Like Computers*. New York: Ferguson, 2010. Print.

Remick, Pat. 21 *Things Every Future Engineer Should Know: A Practical Guide for Students and Parents*. Chicago: Kaplan AEC Educational, 2006. Print.

Sande, Warren. *Hello World! Computer Programming for Kids and Other Beginners*. Greenwich, CT: Manning, 2009. Print.

WEB LINKS

To learn more about engineering jobs, visit ABDO Publishing Company online at **www.abdopublishing.com**. Web sites about engineering jobs are featured on our Book Links page. These links are routinely monitored and updated to provide the most current information available.

SOURCE NOTES

CHAPTER 1. IS AN ENGINEERING JOB FOR YOU?

1. "Quotes." *CV Engineering.* CV Engineering, 2009. Web. 17 June 2010.

2. "Engineering." *Merriam Webster.* Merriam Webster, Inc., 2010. Web. 28 June 2010.

3. "Volunteer Community Service." *American Society of Civil Engineers.* American Society of Civil Engineers, n.d. Web. 17 June 2010.

4. U.S. Bureau of Labor Statistics. "Engineers." *Occupational Outlook Handbook, 2010–11 Edition.* U.S. Bureau of Labor Statistics, 17 Dec. 2009. Web. 20 July 2010.

CHAPTER 2. WHAT IS A CHEMICAL ENGINEER?

1. "Welcome to MIT ChemE." *Department of Chemical Engineering.* Massachusetts Institute of Technology, Department of Engineering, 2010. Web. 29 June 2010.

2. "Where Do Chemical Engineers Work?" *Chemical Engineering.* Department of Chemical Engineering, Worcester Polytechnic Institute, 22 May 2008. Web. 29 June 2010.

3. Ibid.

4. U.S. Bureau of Labor Statistics. "Engineers." *Occupational Outlook Handbook, 2010–11 Edition.* U.S. Bureau of Labor Statistics, 17 Dec. 2009. Web. 28 June 2010.

5. "NACE Research: Salary Survey's Top Employers by Average Salary Offer, Number of Offers." *NACE.* National Association of College and Employers, n.d. Web. 28 June 2010.

6. Jennifer Wegerer. "Chemical Engineering." *AllEngineeringSchools.* All Star Directions, Inc., 2010. Web. 6 Oct. 2010.

7. U.S. Bureau of Labor Statistics. "Engineers." *Occupational Outlook Handbook, 2010–11 Edition.* U.S. Bureau of Labor Statistics, 17 Dec. 2009. Web. 6 Oct. 2010.

8. Jason Trask. Interview by Susan E. Hamen. 16 July 2010.

9. Ibid.

10. Ibid.

11. "Pure Fun: Ivory Floating Soap Legend." *Ivory.* Procter & Gamble, 2009. Web. 30 June 2010.

12. "Chemical Engineering Branch." *United States Environmental Protection Agency.* Environmental Protection Agency, 22 Apr. 2010. Web. 30 June 2010.

CHAPTER 3. WOULD YOU MAKE A GOOD CHEMICAL ENGINEER?

1. "Meet Our Students." *Department of Chemical Engineering*. Massachusetts Institute of Technology, Department of Engineering, 2010. Web. 29 June 2010.

2. Lynn Reuvers. Interview by Susan E. Hamen. 21 June 2010.

CHAPTER 4. WHAT IS AN ENVIRONMENTAL ENGINEER?

1. Mike Pflanz. "World Water Day: Dirty Water Kills More People Than Violence, Says UN." *The Christian Science Monitor*. The Christian Science Monitor, 22 Mar. 2010. Web. 2 July 2010.

2. U.S. Bureau of Labor Statistics. "Engineers." *Occupational Outlook Handbook, 2010–11 Edition*. U.S. Bureau of Labor Statistics, 17 Dec. 2009. Web. 28 June 2010.

3. Ibid.

4. Anne Fisher. "Hot Careers for the Next 10 Years." *CNNMoney*. Cable News Network, 21 March 2005. Web. 5 July 2010.

5. George Beatty. Interview by Susan E. Hamen. 30 June 2010.

6. Ibid.

7. Ibid.

8. Campbell Robertson and Leslie Kaufman. "Size of Spill in Gulf of Mexico Is Larger than Thought." *The New York Times*. The New York Times Company, 28 Apr. 2010. Web. 6. Oct. 2010.

9. Alan Silverleib. "The Gulf Spill: America's Worst Environmental Disaster?" *CNN U.S.* Cable News Network, 10 Aug. 2010. Web. 20 Aug. 2010.

10. Christopher Harrington. Interview by Susan E. Hamen. 21 July 2010.

CHAPTER 5. WOULD YOU MAKE A GOOD ENVIRONMENTAL ENGINEER?

1. "Careers: Opportunities for Students." *United States Environmental Protection Agency*. Environmental Protection Agency, n.d. Web. 6 Oct. 2010.

2. P. Aarne Vesilind, J. Jeffrey Peirce, and Ruth F. Weiner. *Environmental Engineering*. Newton, MA: Butterworth-Heinemann, 2003. Print. 10.

3. "A 'Day in the life' of a DNR...." *Iowa Department of Natural Resources*. Iowa Department of Natural Resources, n.d. Web. 15 July 2010.

SOURCE NOTES CONTINUED

CHAPTER 6. WHAT IS A COMPUTER ENGINEER?

1. Jonathan Mueller. Interview by Susan E. Hamen. 17 July 2010.

2. U.S. Bureau of Labor Statistics. "Computer Software Engineers and Computer Programmers." *Occupational Outlook Handbook, 2010–11 Edition.* U.S. Bureau of Labor Statistics, 17 Dec. 2009. Web. 6 Oct. 2010.

3. U.S. Bureau of Labor Statistics. "Engineers." *Occupational Outlook Handbook, 2010–11 Edition.* U.S. Bureau of Labor Statistics, 17 Dec. 2009. Web. 28 June 2010.

4. U.S. Bureau of Labor Statistics. "Computer Software Engineers and Computer Programmers." *Occupational Outlook Handbook, 2010–11 Edition.* U.S. Bureau of Labor Statistics, 17 Dec. 2009. Web. 6 Oct. 2010.

5. U.S. Bureau of Labor Statistics. "Engineers." *Occupational Outlook Handbook, 2010–11 Edition.* U.S. Bureau of Labor Statistics, 17 Dec. 2009. Web. 28 June 2010.

6. U.S. Bureau of Labor Statistics. "Computer Software Engineers and Computer Programmers." *Occupational Outlook Handbook, 2010–11 Edition.* U.S. Bureau of Labor Statistics, 17 Dec. 2009. Web. 6 Oct. 2010.

7. U.S. Bureau of Labor Statistics. "Engineers." *Occupational Outlook Handbook, 2010–11 Edition.* U.S. Bureau of Labor Statistics, 17 Dec. 2009. Web. 28 June 2010.

8. U.S. Bureau of Labor Statistics. "Computer Software Engineers and Computer Programmers." *Occupational Outlook Handbook, 2010–11 Edition.* U.S. Bureau of Labor Statistics, 17 Dec. 2009. Web. 6 Oct. 2010.

9. U.S. Bureau of Labor Statistics. "Engineers." *Occupational Outlook Handbook, 2010–11 Edition.* U.S. Bureau of Labor Statistics, 17 Dec. 2009. Web. 28 June 2010.

10. Jourdan Bennett. Interview by Susan E. Hamen. 8 Sept. 2010.

11. Ibid.

CHAPTER 7. WOULD YOU MAKE A GOOD COMPUTER ENGINEER?

1. Chip Chick. "Introducing Computer Engineer Barbie! Barbie Unveils Her 125th &126th Careers." *Chip Chick.* Chip Chick, 12 Feb. 2010. Web. 12 Aug. 2010.

2. "Best Engineering Schools." *USNews.com.* U.S. News & World Report Online, n.d. Web. 7 Sept. 2010.

CHAPTER 8. WHAT IS A VIDEO GAME DEVELOPER?

1. "2010 Sales, Demographic and Usage: Essential Facts about the Computer and Video Game Industry." *Entertainment Software Association*. ESA Entertainment Software Association, 2010. Web. 30 July 2010.

2. Ibid.

3. "Summary Report for: 15-1099.13 - Video Game Designers." *O*NET Online*. O*NET, n.d. Web. 30 June 2010.

4. Ibid.

5. Brian Colin. Interview by Susan E. Hamen. 26 July 2010.

6. "Game Designers' First Jobs." *YouTube*. N.p., 20 Nov. 2007. Web. 24 Sept. 2010.

7. Brian Colin. Interview by Susan E. Hamen. 26 July 2010.

8. Ibid.

CHAPTER 9. WOULD YOU MAKE A GOOD VIDEO GAME DEVELOPER?

1. Mike Snider. "USC Ranked No. 1 among Video-Game Design Programs." *USA Today*. USA Today, 28 Feb. 2010. Web. 30 June 2010.

2. Kristin Kalning. "Sure, It's a Cool Job. But Do Games Pay?" *MSNBC.com*. MSNBC.com, 5 May 2007. Web. 6 Oct. 2010.

3. Brian Colin. Interview by Susan E. Hamen. 26 July 2010.

4. Ibid.

5. "Summary Report for: 15-1099.13 - Video Game Designers." *O*NET Online*. O*NET, n.d. Web. 30 June 2010.

6. Kristin Kalning. "Sure, It's a Cool Job. But Do Games Pay?" *MSNBC.com*. MSNBC.com, 5 May 2007. Web. 6 Oct. 2010.

INDEX

Advanced Placement classes, 30, 49, 72

aerospace engineer, 10

aqueducts, 7

Babbage, Charles, 67

Beatty, George, 39–40

Bennett, Jourdan, 59–61

British Petroleum Deepwater Horizon, 40

Byron, August Ada, 67

chemical engineer, 10, 14–33, 50
    education, 30–33
    handling by-products, 17
    safety procedures, 16–17
    skills, 26–29
    specializations, 15
    wages, 19
    work environment, 17, 19

CHS Oilseed Processing and Refining, 20

civil engineer, 7, 11, 12, 35, 37, 42, 50

Colin, Brian, 81–83, 93

computer engineer, 10, 54–74, 77
    central processing unit, 56
    computer graphic animation software, 73
    education, 72–74
    operating system, 55, 56, 58
    skills, 66–71
    specializations, 55–57
    wages, 58
    work environment, 58

Computer Engineer Barbie, 68

da Vinci, Leonardo, 8

Department of Labor, US, 38, 58

Egyptian pyramids, 7

electrical engineer, 11, 56, 64, 65

electronics engineer, 11

Entertainment Software Association, 78

environmental engineer, 10, 34–42
    education, 48–52
    groundwater monitoring, 36
    hazardous waste, 35
    skills, 44–48
    specializations, 36
    wages, 38
    water treatment, 35, 36
    women and minorities, 51
    work environment, 36–37

Environmental Protection Agency, US, 22

Fortune magazine, 38

Game Developer Magazine, 80

Game Refuge, 82, 93

Garriott, Richard, 82

Great Wall of China, 7

Greek Parthenon, 7

health and safety engineer, 11

industrial engineer, 11, 12
Ivory soap, 21

Junior Engineering Technical Society, 72

Lee, Gabe, 50
LG Electronics, 60

Massachusetts Institute of Technology, 15, 72
    Department of Chemical Engineering, 15
materials engineer, 11–12
mechanical engineer, 12, 39, 56, 62
Miller, Christine, 94
MSNBC.com, 94
Mueller, Jonathan, 56

National Oceanic and Atmospheric Administration, 40
Nauman, Jeff, 82
nuclear engineer, 12

Obama, Barack, 40

petroleum engineer, 12
Proctor & Gamble, 21

Reuvers, Lynn, 32

Southern Illinois University, 81
Stanford University, 72

Trask, Jason, 19–21

United Nations Environment Programme, 36
U.S. News & World Report, 72

video game developer, 10, 76–94
    design document, 92
    education, 92–94
    skills, 88–91
    wages, 80
    work environment, 79–80

ABOUT THE AUTHOR

Susan E. Hamen has written educational children's books on a variety of topics. She lives in her home state, Minnesota, with her husband and two children.

PHOTO CREDITS